Understa
Financial Crisis of 2008

By Aiden Young

Understanding the Financial Crisis of 2008

Copyright © 2016 C&D Publications

All Rights Reserved. No part of this book may be reproduced in any form without written permission from the author. Reviewers may quote brief passages in reviews.

Table of Contents

Introduction 1

Chapter 1: Deregulation of Wall Street 3

Chapter 2: Impact of Lowered Interest Rates   7

Chapter 3: Shadow Banking System 11

Chapter 4: Housing Market: 15

Chapter 5: Mortgage Standards 19

Chapter 6: What Happened in 2007 and 2008? 23

Chapter 7: Bank Bailouts and Their Impact 27

Chapter 8: Current and Future Economic Climate 33

Chapter 9: Cultural Impact of the Financial Crisis 37

Chronology of Events 41

Glossary of Financial Terms 45

Acknowledgments 53

About the Author 55

Additional Books by Aiden Young 57

Index 59

Introduction

The global financial crisis of 2007 and 2008 is widely recognized as the worst such crisis to impact the world's economy since the Great Depression in the 1930s. Massive financial institutions went bust while others were only saved by government bailouts. Many companies went bankrupt, most notably those engaged in the mortgage industry. Consumer health and confidence fell down to incredible lows while millions of people in the United States lost their homes in 2007, 2008 and 2009.

While most of the events in this financial crisis took place in 2007 and 2008, the roots of the crisis can date back to a few decades. From the deregulation of Wall Street and mortgage companies to the predatory actions of those companies, there is a lot of blame to go around for this crisis. Some blame the government for relaxing their rules while others blame the major banks and hedge funds on Wall Street for their careless speculation and enormous greed.

In reality, every economic bubble is met with an eventual bust. The United States housing market was experiencing an enormous bubble, with many factors combining to ensure that people had access to more loans than ever before. When this bubble burst, it triggered a domino effect that impacted every financial institution in the country. And as the world's economies saw the crisis unfold in the United States, they began to experience similar problems of their own. By the end of 2008, we were in a global recession that threatened every facet of the world economy.

Despite measures by world governments to halt the crisis in 2008 and 2009, the global recession did not end until 2012. Even in 2009, when most bank bailouts had passed and things looked slightly better, most first world countries experienced GDP growth rates of 0 to -10 percent. Of the major nations in the world, only China and India experienced a GDP growth in 2009. GDP refers to the total value of all goods and services produced in a specific period of time, and economists believe it is one of the best ways to measure the health of a nation's economy.

From a numbers perspective, the crisis and recession are over. The global financial markets are healthy, investment in various sectors is much higher than the 2007 to 2012 levels, and major companies around the world are doing very well for themselves. However, the impact of the crisis is far from washed away, especially for the general public. The job market is healthier than the 2008-2012 period, but it is still not great.

Meanwhile, confidence in Wall Street and the financial markets is at an all-time low, with many people around the world blaming the greed of bankers on a worldwide crisis that saw them lose their homes, their jobs and everything they had worked so hard to obtain.

With this book, we attempt to clarify the causes of the financial crisis, the key players that contributed to the crisis and how this crisis unfolded. We also explain the complex financial terms and schemes that eventually led to a global financial meltdown.

Chapter 1: Deregulation of Wall Street

"The choice is between which mistake is easier to correct: underdoing it or overdoing it." - Timothy Geithner, Former United States Secretary of the Treasury

Many prominent economists, such as Paul Krugman and Timothy Geithner, believe that the regulation from the United States government towards the financial industry did not keep up with the industry's innovation. With things such as the shadow banking system, derivatives, and off-balance sheet financing gaining popularity, the government took little action to regulate these systems.

Derivatives refer to financial instruments where the price of the security depends on the performance of the underlying assets within the agreement. Derivatives can include stocks, bonds, currencies or even interest rates. Investors use derivatives in order to hedge against their other investments, or to speculate on certain assets.

If we are to take a serious look at the deregulation of Wall Street, we can trace its roots all the way back to the 1980s. It was Jimmy Carter and the Depository Institutions Deregulation and Monetary Control Act in 1980 that removed a lot of restrictions that regulated banks and their financial practices. It allowed them increased lending powers, legalized credit unions and even raised the deposit insurance limit to $100,000 from the previous $40,000. The deposit insurance limit is relevant because it resulted in depositors lowering their level of scrutiny regarding a lender's risk management practices.

Ronald Reagan followed up this move with the Garn – St. Germain Depository Institutions Act in 1982. This ensured that adjustable-rate mortgage loans were legal while also lowering regulation on other aspects of banking.

From a political point of view, people often argue that the "other side" is largely responsible for catering to the wishes of banks and financial institutions. Unfortunately, history shows us that deregulation of Wall Street is a very bi-partisan issue. Even in the 1990s, Bill Clinton signed a number of laws that lowered regulation on banks, but no one noticed because the country's economy was flourishing.

Clinton approved the Gramm – Leach – Bliley Act in 1999 that removed provisions from the Glass-Steagall Act. The purpose of this act was to split the banks between investment banking and commercial banking. It was enacted in the 1930s, ironically after another financial crisis, in response to many improper banking activities. Experts felt that commercial banks were taking too many risks with the money deposited in the hope of huge rewards. Instead of focusing on their commercial side and providing great services to the public, they were more worried about how much money they could make by investing that money in riskier and riskier areas.

There is a lot of public perception that the Glass-Steagal Act's repeal played a huge role in the financial crisis. To some extent, it is true, because commercial banks were heavily involved in risky investments that led to problems in 2007 and 2008. However, a high percentage of the institutions that felt the brunt of the financial crisis were NOT under the jurisdiction of this act. For example, the insurance company AIG, Fannie Mae, Freddie Mac and a number of other institutions.

A final piece of regulation that really impacted the financial crisis is the relaxation of the net capital rule by the United States Securities and Exchange Commission, or SEC, 2004. The SEC is responsible for enforcing federal laws pertaining to the financial industry.

Figure - United States Securities and Exchange Commission Seal

With the net capital rule relaxed, major and minor investment banks throughout the country were able to increase how much debt they took on for investments. Because of this increased level of debt, mortgage-backed securities became a lot more popular, which in turn increased the volume of subprime mortgages.

This term, mortgage-backed security, gained a lot of exposure during the crisis. However, so many people did not have the faintest idea how to understand the concept behind these securities. Here is a simple explanation of the mortgage-backed security:

A mortgage-backed security is a type of investment that is backed up by one or more mortgages.

This means that someone investing in a mortgage-backed security is indirectly lending money to a person or business so they can buy residential or commercial properties. The reason why this type of security got so popular is because it allowed smaller banks to offer mortgages to customers without caring whether they could pay back the mortgage. If the customer failed to pay, it was the mortgage-backed security's investors that were in trouble, not the smaller bank.

These securities were given ratings by credit agencies, which signified the quality of the mortgage. In theory, a mortgage-backed security filled with high-risk mortgages should have a very low credit rating. However, this was not always the case, as we will explain a little later.

Subprime mortgages refer to mortgages made out to people who may not have the credit rating to justify a traditional loan. The interest rate on these mortgages was a lot higher than a conventional mortgage. If you had a credit rating below 600 or had declared bankruptcy any time in the past, you were dependent on a subprime mortgage to buy a home.

Chapter 2: Impact of Lowered Interest Rates

"If the fiscal cliff occurs, I don't think the Federal Reserve has the tools to offset that event." - Ben Bernanke, former chairman of the Federal Reserve

Over a four-year period from 2000 to 2003, the United States Federal Reserve reduced the target federal funds rate from 6.5 percent to 1 percent. This drastic lowering of the rate coincided with the dot com bubble's collapse, along with the September 11 terrorist attacks in 2001. At the time, the Federal Reserve also had concerns regarding the possibility of deflation in the United States economy.

While a majority of the population was shocked when the 2007-2008 Financial Crisis started with the crash of the housing markets, economists were predicting that the housing market was in a bubble way back in 2002. In fact, they stated that it might be a good idea for the economy to replace the dot-com bubble with a "housing bubble." The Dot-com bubble refers to the huge gains made by internet and technology stocks from 1997-2000.

Credit was the main reason why so many people were buying houses, and this stretched for more than five years prior to the crisis. Another reason why interest rates kept decreasing was the fact that the United States was operating at a record deficit for their current accounts. This meant that they were reliant on borrowing money from foreign countries. This constant borrowing meant that bond prices kept rising while interest rates were furthered lowered.

Ben Bernanke, chairman of the Federal Reserve from 2006 to 2014, spoke about the fact that the United States saw their current account deficit rise from 1.5 percent of the nation's GDP to 5.8 percent. In numerical terms, this was an increase of $650 billion. In order to keep their books balanced, the United States had no choice but to keep borrowing money from foreign countries that had trade surpluses, such as China.

Figure – Ben Bernanke, former chairman of the Federal Reserve

Understanding the Financial Crisis of 2008

When a nation borrows a lot of money from other sources, the identity of its balance of payments necessitates that they ensure their capital account's surplus is equivalent to the deficit in their current account. In order to maintain this balance, the United States had a great deal of foreign money coming into the country to finance their various imports.

With so much foreign money coming into the country during those years, it meant that the demand for financial assets was at an all-time high. Increased demand means higher prices for the assets, along with lower interest rates. Bernanke referred to this increased asset demand as the "savings glut." Essentially, a lot of people in foreign countries, especially China, had a lot of money saved and needed places to invest it.

As this foreign capital kept pouring into the United States, it was going to a variety of places. Foreign governments put these funds in the United States through purchases of Treasury bonds. Ironically, this helped them avoid a lot of the financial crisis' impact. Unfortunately, United States households did not have the same luck. They used the funds borrowed from foreign investors to finance their consumption through increased credit lines. This increased credit also meant that people were building more and more for houses, raising their prices and contributing to the housing bubble. Meanwhile, financial institutions in the United States invested most of this money into mortgage-backed securities.

The initial declines in the interest rate certainly contributed to the financial crisis, because they laid the ground work for people to buy homes at ridiculous prices. Also, they prompted banks to engage in borderline-illegal practices in order to continue giving people more credit. However, another move by the Federal Reserve is probably what accelerated the start of the crisis: the increase in interest rates from 2004 to 2006.

During those three years, the Fed decided to increase interest rates significantly. As a result, basic mortgage interest rates became more expensive for homeowners. This resulted in the increased popularity of the adjustable-rate mortgage, or ARM, rates. Because people could not afford the higher interest rate, banks used the ARM rates to start people off at a lower rate, with the stipulation that it would increase after one or five years. A lot of these ARM rates fell under the umbrella of predatory lending.

Chapter 3: Shadow Banking System

"There is a very real danger that financial regulation will become a wolf in sheep's clothing." Henry "Hank" Paulson, former Secretary of the Treasury

When people talk about the shadow banking system, they are usually referring to the action of intermediators in the financial system who help create credit for various institutions. This type of shadow banking is not regulated, which means that it can lead to problematic actions. Sometimes regulated institutions also engage in unregulated behavior, which includes them in the shadow banking system.

One reason why shadow banking never received regulation is because traditional bank deposits were not used to move the money. This meant that financial institutions could use shadow banking to take on more risks and gain higher levels of credit. But these investments did not need to meet the regulated capital requirements for the subsequent investments. An aspect of shadow banking that did a lot of damage in this financial crisis was the credit default swap or CDS.

A credit default swap is designed to allow one financial party to obtain insurance on the credit line they have given out. For example, let's say financial 'Institution A' lends $500,000 to a borrower. If they are worried about the borrower's ability to pay back this money, they might want to get a CDS from 'Institution B'. However, 'Institution B' says they will only provide this insurance if they are paid $10,000 a year.

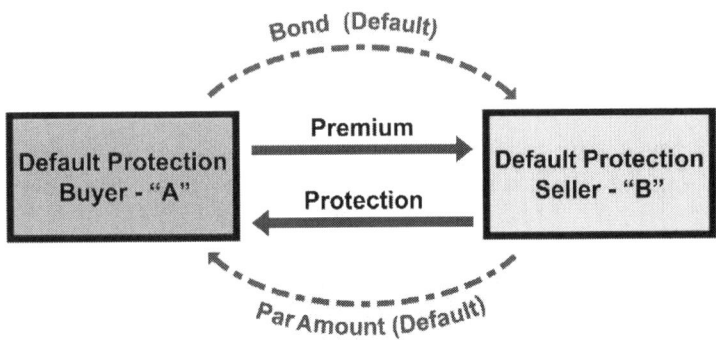

Figure – Simplified Credit Default Swap Diagram

What is the benefit of a credit default swap for either party? In this sample case, 'Institution A' gets assurances from 'institution B' that if the borrower defaults on the loan, 'Institution B' will cover the costs. On the flipside, 'Institution B' believes that the borrower has a solid credit and will pay back the loan, which means they are getting $10,000 a year for providing insurance they do not believe will ever be needed.

The problem arises when 'Institution B' gets into financial trouble. If they no longer have the ability to insure the borrower's debt, it means that 'Institution A' is now in trouble as well. Because of 'Institution B' and their inability to keep their end of the deal, 'Institution A' now has a bunch of unsecured debt, which puts credit agencies on notice. Maybe 'Institution A' had a triple A rating in terms of its reliability, but this bunch of unsecured debt may cause the credit agency to downgrade them.

While this simple example shows how a CDS works, it does not even begin to explain the complex way that financial institutions used this device in order to place bets on other debt and even other financial institutions. If we go back to our example, we can now add 'Institution C', which has decided to use a CDS to bet on the failure of 'Institution B'.

Here is one statistic that should give everyone pause with regards to the absurd way that the financial markets abused shadow banking and the credit default swaps: The Bank of International Settlements reported that around one QUADRILLION dollars' worth of derivatives trading took place. One quadrillion is 1,000 trillion dollars. Meanwhile, the GDP of every country on planet Earth combined is only 60 trillion dollars. This shows that financial gamblers were able to bet on whatever they wanted, with however much money they wanted, thanks to the lack of regulation on shadow banking and derivatives.

Chapter 4: Housing Market:

"The financial crisis should not become an excuse to raise taxes, which would only undermine the economic growth required to regain our strength." George W. Bush, former President of the United States

We all know that the United States housing market experienced an incredible boom in the years leading up to the financial crisis. With a look at some of the numbers, we can see just how big this boom had become. Between 1998 and 2006, an average home in the United States saw its price increase by 125 percent. The price of a home from 1981 to 2001 ranged from between 2.9 to 3.1 times the median household income at the time. This is a fairly steady number, showing that housing prices were rising with increased income and inflation.

However, by 2004 this ratio reached 4. By 2006, it was at 4.6. It was clear that people were not buying these extraordinarily expensive homes because they were making much more money in 2004 to 2006 than they were in the late 90s or early 2000s. This increased investment in housing was coming in the form of relaxed credit standards.

Homeowners were refinancing their existing mortgages at lower rates while many were taking out second or third mortgages in order to spend more money elsewhere. It was not uncommon for a family to take out a second mortgage in order to upgrade their home, send a kid to college or even give themselves some spending money to keep in the bank. With interests this low, and banks so willing to lend huge amounts, it was no wonder that everyone took advantage of this situation.

In a special, award-winning program from a number of National Public Radio, or NPR, correspondents, it was highlighted that around $70 trillion in fixed income investments throughout the world were desiring higher yields than those you get from the United States treasury bonds. This was happening in the early to mid-2000s. Referred to as a "Giant Pool of Money," this meant that there was a section of the financial industry responsible for this massive increase in higher yield investments.

With traditional income generating investments remaining relatively stagnant, experts looked for the sector responsible for the higher yield investments. As it turns out, it was the housing market answering people's demand for higher yield with their investments. Thanks to mortgage-backed securities and collateralized debt obligations, the housing market was a huge pool of money for the financial markets. We can add mortgage brokers, small banks, investment banks and other institutions into this umbrella because they all stood to gain in one way or another.

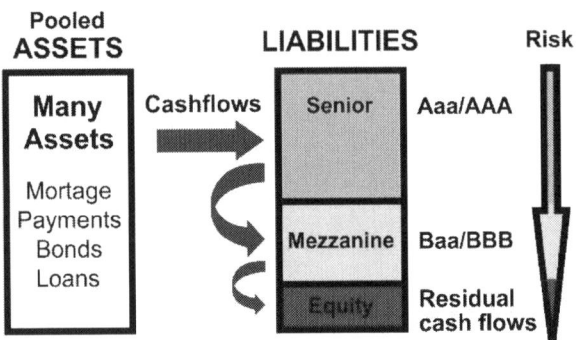

Figure – Collateralized Debt Obligation (CDO) Simplified Diagram

Understanding the Financial Crisis of 2008

What is a collateralized debt obligation, or a CDO? These are complex financial products that are generated by combining various assets that generate cash flow. These assets are repackaged and sold to investors. It is referred to as a collateralized debt obligation because all the elements that make up the CDO, such as mortgages, bonds or loans, are debt obligations serving as the CDO's collateral.

Who was involved in the creation of these CDOs? Securities firms, CDO managers, ratings agencies, financial guarantors and investors.

Securities firms were responsible for approving these CDOs and overseeing their creation, along with grouping them into tranches, or portions, based on the risk profile of each CDO. The CDO managers were responsible for selecting the collateral that went into each obligation. Rating agencies gave a credit rating to each CDO, signifying to investors whether a CDO was relatively safe or risky. Guarantors were on hand to ensure investors that they would cover any losses occurred if the CDO collapse. And finally, investors bought the CDOs, and these were usually pension funds, investment banks, and hedge funds.

CDOs have always been a part of the United States economy. However, their increased popularity and use is what helped trigger the financial collapse. From 2003 to 2006, the sales of CDOs in the economy increased from roughly $30 billion to $225 billion. It was these CDOs that allowed financial institutions to give out subprime mortgages and other risky methods of lending because they were using investor funds to do so. When the housing market collapsed, and people began defaulting on their mortgages, most of these CDOs collapsed, with their investors getting nothing in return.

Chapter 5: Mortgage Standards

"Millions of Americans were duped by the federal government and the Federal Reserve into buying homes they could not afford and failed to count the cost. When the financial crisis of 2008 hit, they could not keep up the monthly mortgage payments and defaulted." Mark Skousen, Economist

With the housing market steadily on the rise throughout the 90s, it meant an increase in competition among mortgage lenders. Instead of having strict policies and making it difficult for people to get a mortgage, every lender wanted as many clients as possible. This meant allowing mortgages for people with weaker credit, along with relaxing their underwriting standards.

Up till 2003, mortgage companies were held to task by government-sponsored enterprises or GSEs. These institutions were the policemen of mortgage companies, ensuring that they did not let their standards slip and allow too many people to afford mortgages. Unfortunately, following 2003 the market shifted with the entrance of many private securitizers, which undermined the influence of GSEs. There was so much pressure among securitizers to gain a market share and have additional clients, which meant that they were willing to turn a blind eye to the actions of the mortgage companies they should have been policing.

A vast majority of the terrible loans given out for buying houses and commercial property came between 2004 and 2007 when these standards slipped. This is a classic example of why increased government regulation and presence in an industry is not a bad thing. Instead of letting the government continue to police mortgage companies, the county went with a private solution that turned out to be a catastrophic disaster.

That is not to say that GSEs are blameless from this crisis. Two examples of GSEs are Fannie Mae and Freddie Mac. In order to compete with the private securitizers and banks who were policing mortgage standards in a relaxed manner, they also lowered their standards and stopped doing their jobs properly. There are also those who believe that the actions of these institutions, dating back to 1994, helped cause the crisis.

However, minority and majority reports from the United States Congress showed that, in general, loans from GSEs performed much better than those securitized by private investment banks or other institutions. A few prominent economics, such as Paul Krugman, even claim that the GSEs never bought a single subprime mortgage, but this claim is very contentious among experts.

Along with the relaxing of the policies meant to keep mortgage companies in check, there were also major problems with the underwriters themselves. An example is Citigroup. Their Business Chief Underwriter, Richard M. Bowen III, gave testimony at the Financial Crisis Inquiry Commission following the events of 2007 and 2008. He admitted that the problem with underwriting standards was industry-wide in the years leading up to the crisis.

Bowen stated that around 60 percent of the mortgages bought by Citi in 2006 were created through defective methods. This means that when the policy was written by a mortgage company, it was not done to the standards required of them. Some mortgages did not even contain all the required policy documents and paperwork. He says this number stretched to 80 percent by 2007.

Clayton Holdings is a company that was responsible for performing due diligence on residential loans throughout the United States and in some European countries. Their findings showed that of the 900,000 mortgages reviewed from 2006 to mid-2007, only 54 percent of these loans met the standards of the originating underwriters. Around 28 percent of those loans failed to meet the minimum standard of any issuer in the country. And the most ridiculous fact of all is that around 40 percent of these loans were then packaged up and sold to investors through mortgage-backed securities and CDOs.

A number of practices by mortgage companies and banks during this time fell under the umbrella of predatory lending, which refers to the practice of a lender giving out money to borrowers in a method that is both unsafe and unsound. These lenders were enticing borrowers into getting into loan agreements because they wanted to increase the potential profits for their company, and their actions were definitely not in the borrowers' best interests.

Countrywide Financial is one example of a company that used such techniques to sell people more mortgages. They offered loans with low advertised interest rates, encouraging homeowners to refinance their loans with Countrywide Financial. The loans included complex documents, with the borrower, told that their interest rate was between one to two percent.

However, these borrowers were placed in what we know as the adjustable-rate mortgage. Some of these loans even included the possibility of the borrower making "interest only payments" in some months. This meant that the borrower was never putting a dent into their principal amount, and the interest rate was set to rise exponentially as soon as the adjustable-rate period kicked in.

As the housing market started its downward trajectory in mid-2007 onwards, it left homeowners with no incentive to pay back these mortgages. They were stuck on high-interest rates, with a principal amount higher than their home's worth. This is what caused many companies, such as Countrywide Financial, to collapse thanks to their own terrible underwriting policies.

Employees from other companies, such as Ameriquest, later spoke about how they were encouraged by their bosses to falsify mortgage documents when selling these mortgages to banks on Wall Street. Since the banks were so eager to buy these mortgages, they never bothered to do their due diligence on the paperwork. This mortgage fraud played a significant role in the crisis.

Chapter 6: What Happened in 2007 and 2008?

"Washington's answer to a self-inflicted financial crisis reminded Americans why they so deeply distrust the political class. The 'fiscal cliff' process was secretive and sloppy, and the nation's so-called leadership lacked the political courage to address our root problems: joblessness and debt."
- Ron Fournier, Journalist

All of the events and decisions we mention in the previous chapters culminated in 2007 and 2008 when the worst of the financial crisis hit the United States and the rest of the world. In fact, some trouble began towards the end of 2004. Home ownership in the United States was now at 70 percent, which was its highest point. By the time we got to the last quarter of 2005, home prices were starting to fall. Despite the easy access to mortgages, people were not buying homes with the same fervor and intensity as previous years.

The United States Home Construction Index, which is composed of companies and entities in the home construction business, fell around 40 percent in 2006. This showed that fewer people were buying new homes, which meant construction of those homes had slowed down. However, this was not the only problem. In 2006, the first raft of subprime mortgage borrowers were starting to struggle with their loans. Their adjustable-rate had kicked in, which meant they were now paying a lot more interest than before.

2007 was probably the worst year of the crisis, at least for most of the country. People were defaulting on their homes left, right and center, with so many individuals and families forced to leave their family homes and look for a new place to live. From a corporate point of view, mortgage lenders were filing for bankruptcy by the month, with subprime and adjustable-rate mortgage lenders hit the worst. February and March of 2007 alone saw 25 subprime mortgage lenders file for bankruptcy. By April, the biggest known subprime lender, New Century Financial, was also ready to call it quits.

Figure – Homes in Foreclosure

This is when the panic started. People were starting to read about subprime mortgages in the news, along with horror stories of their neighbors, friends, and family who had no choice but to vacate their homes because they could not keep up with the payments.

The news media was also starting to pick up on the mortgage-backed securities and CDOs related to these subprime mortgages. Financial instructions such as hedge funds now owed close to a trillion dollars in these worthless securities. If the subprime borrowers started defaulting in mass, which was already happening, these financial companies were teetering on the edge of disaster.

Bear Stearns close two of their subprime mortgage-related hedge funds in June, while Merrill Lynch seized around $800 million in assets from those two hedge funds. At the time, we thought this might be the worst of it. But this was only the beginning.

The landslide occurred in August 2007 when it was abundantly clear that no one in the financial sector had a solution to the subprime mortgage crisis. Problems were now filtering towards Europe and Asia as well. A major British bank, Northern Rock, had to go to the Bank of England in an attempt to get a loan to solve their liquidity issues. The world's central banks and governments were busy trying to formulate strategies to mitigate and reverse the damage already caused by the crisis.

By September 2008, the average house price in the United States was around 20 percent lower than the mid-2006 levels. Prices were going down, which meant that it was impossible for homeowners to refinance their adjustable-rate mortgages. Since the higher payments were something they could not afford, many defaulted on their loans.

We now know that roughly 1.3 million properties were foreclosed by lenders in 2007, which marked a massive 75 percent increase from 2006. But this number only got worse: there were 2.3 million foreclosures in 2008 and many more in 2009. In August 2008, almost 10 percent of all mortgages in the United States were delinquent or foreclosed. This number rose to 15 percent in September 2009.

The problems were exacerbated by the fact that the housing crisis and subprime mortgage problems started a financial tsunami that was impacting every financial institution in the world. Banks had liquidity problems, investment banks were buried in debt they had no way of paying off and mortgage lenders were all but out of business. The interbank market, which is a foreign exchange market where banks trade in currencies, was also on the verge of collapse, which had a huge impact on the global stock exchange and financial markets.

The United States Federal Reserve was doing its best to stop the damage in 2008, by slashing its discount rate and federal funds rate. However, this had no impact compared to the bad news coming from various financial sectors. Lehman Brothers and Indymac Bank both collapsed while JP Morgan Chase took over Bear Sterns. Merill Lynch was now in Bank of America's hands while the United States government now owned Fannie Mae and Freddie Mac.

These rate cuts were not limited to the United States. While their Federal funds rate and discount rate was at 1 percent and 1.75 percent, the same cuts were seen throughout Europe and Asia. The central banks in England, Canada, China and Switzerland, all engaged in enormous rate cuts to try and help their financial institutions. But increasing liquidity was not enough to stop a full-blown recession.

While it was an unpopular move with the general public, the United States National Economic Stabilization Act of 2008, commonly referred to as a bailout of the U.S. financial system, is thought by many to be the one event that halted the recession and got the world's economy on a gradual slide towards normalcy.

If we are to learn anything from this financial crisis, it is that our world is so interconnected in these matters. It is no longer possible to look at the financial fate of one country and be secure in the knowledge that such problems will not come your way. The housing crisis may have been an exclusive problem for the United States, but the dominoes that fell from this event caused the entire world's economy to come to its knees.

Chapter 7: Bank Bailouts and Their Impact

"We talk about institutions that are too big to fail - I think the story is as much about people who think they are too big to fail." - Andrew Ross Sorkin, Journalist

The United States enacted the Emergency Economic Stabilization Act in October 2008. The act came in response to the financial crisis of 2007 and 2008, with the government bailing out a number of major banks, financial institutions, and other companies. The act, which made its way through Congress and received the President's signature, allowed the United States Secretary of the Treasury to finance around $700 billion in recovery actions. The government bought a number of distressed assets, such as the mortgage-backed securities or CDOs, and gave this money to the banks in order to help their situation at the time.

While there are many criticisms of the bailout, here are some facts that can help us understand why the government felt that action was unavoidable:

On October 6th, 2008, the world's economy was in complete meltdown. The DOW Jones dropped 700 points in a single day, going below its 10,000 figure for the first time in almost half a decade. The FTSE 100 in Britain was 8 percent down while France and Germany's stock markets were in a similar downward spiral. Russia even suspended trading entirely after their stock market fell 20 percent in a single day.

The government's rationale for the bailout stated that they felt this plan was the best way to rescue the world's economy. By offering a bailout to financial institutions, they wanted to create stability in the credit markets. Not only were major banks under threat, but if the credit markets had sunk further, every small business and family in the United States would have been in serious trouble.

Companies across the country, even those not tied to Wall Street, were having serious problems with liquidity. They did not have enough cash on hand to resume their regular activities because the banks that gave them this cash did not have any themselves. Every part of the United States economy was on the verge of collapse if this liquidity crisis continued.

Instead of pushing a smaller plan that would trickle down over many months or years, the United States government felt that swift and dramatic action was necessary. There was no other alternative, especially with the prospect of the recession deepening further. Not only would the bailout help financial institutions, but it would help restore the public's faith in their economy and government.

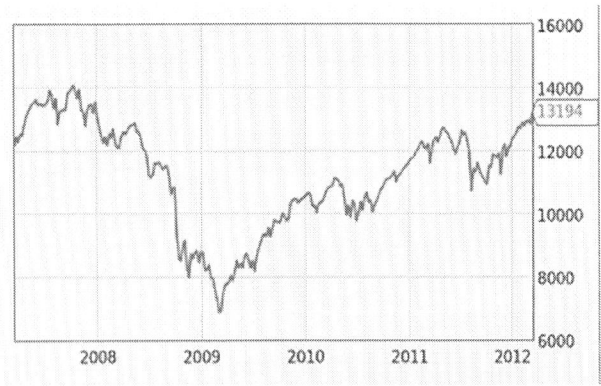

Figure – Dow Jones Industrial Average 2007 to 2012

For those who doubt the impact of this bailout, we only need to look at the stock market's reaction to the first news of a potential bailout. In the middle of September 2008, the first news filtered in that the Treasury had a bailout plan to present to Congress. This saw stock markets in the United States rise slightly while markets around the world surged at the news.

Despite the government's intentions, which appeared genuine, there was a massive outcry by the public at news of a potential Wall Street bailout. With news only out for a week, protests already began in more than 100 cities around the United States. A grassroots organization, TrueMajority, said they organized more than 250 protests in almost each state in the country. Around 1,000 angry protesters made their way to the New York Stock Exchange to express their disappointment at the news.

Interestingly enough, the public's reaction to a possible bailout varied greatly when they were asked the question in a certain manner. A number of pollsters and research centers conducted questionnaires regarding the bailout to gauge public interest.

On the same dates, September 19th to 22nd, Pew, and Bloomberg conducted separate polls asking people whether they favored the bailout. The Pew poll showed 57 percent favored it while the Bloomberg poll showed that only 31 percent were in favor of the bailout.

Why did the numbers vary so much in both polls? Because the Pew poll simply asked if the government should spend money in order to keep the economy and financial markets secure. Meanwhile, the Bloomberg poll asked if people were okay with the government using their tax money in order to bail out financial institutions who caused the economy's collapse in the first place. Understandably, people were less likely to support the bailout when it was put to them in those terms.

For their part, politicians were fairly bi-partisan on the issue. Most Republicans and Democrats in the United States supported the bailout. George Bush signed the first bailout into effect while Barack Obama also supported future plans. Some politicians did put a slightly greater emphasis on trying to ensure that these things did not happen again, especially relative to the mortgage defaults and foreclosure crisis engulfing the nation.

Many economists believed that while the plan had good intentions, it was not the best approach. For example, Paul Krugman stated that the government should have provided the banks with equity in exchange for preferred stock, instead of purchasing the bad assets of those banks. If the government had bought preferred shares, they would have received dividends a few years later, while giving the banks a chance to buy back those shares from the government in the future.

In terms of who received the bailout money, most decisions were based on the size of the institutions and whether they had a good chance of surviving thanks to the money given by the government. If an institution was deemed absolutely necessary to the survival of the economy, it was given a bailout. Similarly, institutions that were in trouble, but had a conceivable plan for recovery were also given assistance.

The biggest and longest-lasting criticism of the government bailout is that it promoted the culture of "too big to fail" among Wall Street and other financial institutions. Instead, many people argued that the government should have made it a necessity for institutions receiving aid to break themselves up into smaller parts. This way, they would not be essential to the economy's survival if a future crisis ever presented itself.

For example, institutions such as Bank of America and Citigroup are certainly "too big to fail," but that would not be the case if they were split up into 10 or 20 different companies each. However, not all economists agree with this criticism. They believe that large institutions, and the resulting economies of scale, in any industry are not necessarily a bad thing. However, they believe that heavy regulation is necessary if there are

Understanding the Financial Crisis of 2008

a number of very large players in any industry.

Economies of scale refer to the cost advantages that a company experiences as they get larger. These cost advantages arise because the company becomes more efficient in whatever industry they are involved.

Those who advocate that "too big to fail" is a problem believe that companies or banks that are so huge they require a bailout can act with this in mind. For example, a bank that knows it is essential to the country or world's economy can keep taking risks with their investments. Even if they fail, the government will bail them out with little to no consequences for the company or its upper management. This promotes the same 'high risk, high reward' investment strategy that caused the crisis in the first place.

Chapter 8: Current and Future Economic Climate

"Food Stamp recipients didn't cause the financial crisis; recklessness on Wall Street did." – President Barack Obama

If we look at the progression of the United States economy from 2011 until 2015, there is a clear indication that things are getting better. In 2011, many people still believed the economy to be in the midst of the financial crisis. While the stock market was vastly improved from the dark days of 2009, the same could not be said for the job market.

The percentage growth of GDP in the United States was 1.6 in 2011, with this number growing to 2.4 percent in 2015. The biggest growth has probably come in the form of consumption, with the figures of 1.6 and 1.7 percent growth from 2011 and 2012 vastly different from the 2.7 and 3.1 percent growth in 2014 and 2015. This shows that people in the United States have more money and are now willing to spend it.

Investments and exports are on the decline, which is not great news while industrial production is still in decline. Most importantly, the unemployment rate was 8.9 percent in 2011 and 8.1 percent in 2012. This figure is now at 5.3 percent and steadily declining. It is not clear whether the new jobs being added are well-paying, but it is still an improvement.

The United States is still the largest economy in the world and commands around 20 percent of the entire global output. Only smaller European countries are able to pass the United States on the figure of per capita GDP, with America in 6th position there. A high number of major corporations are still American, with one-fifth of all companies on the Fortune Global 500 list based in the United States.

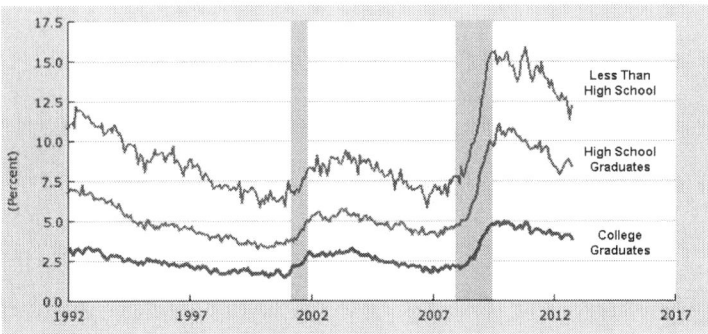

Figure – Unemployment Rate in the United States by education level. Shaded regions are periods of recession.

While the economy is improving, in general, there is still a shift from the manufacturing to a service-based economy. Manufacturing is only 15 percent of the country's current output, with some experts worried that this number will decrease further with impending trade deals and further globalization.

The fastest growing sectors of the United States economy are without a doubt the technology, financial services, retail and healthcare industries. Farming and agriculture make up only two percent of the country's output.

While the financial bailout of Wall Street is now over, with some banks even paying back the government handsomely, there are still active financial policies the government is using to try and further grow the economy. The practice of quantitative easing is in effect in the United States.

Quantitative easing refers to the practices of keeping interest rates low, buying large amounts of financial assets to increase the money supply and ensuring that long-term interest rates also stay down. This policy, along with other factors, show that the economy is far from out of the woods.

As an example, many in the United States are worried about the types of jobs available. Some argue that there are more part-time positions available while the number of full-time jobs with benefits are still not as high as necessary. In addition, the country has a major infrastructure problem, with many roads, tunnels, bridges, trains and highways in need of repairs.

Wages are also stagnating, with income inequality on the rise. Critics of the government and Wall Street believe that the bailout helped ensure that rich people would continue to get richer while the middle class was left to fend for themselves. Medical costs are also increasing while the United States government's deficit remains.

There is hope that the world has learned from the global financial crisis of 2007 and 2008, but it remains to be seen how the next 15 or 20 years will shape up from an economic standpoint. Will we continue to see rising income inequality? Or will the United States and other first world governments make an effort to "level the playing field" so that their middle class can experience a true revival?

Chapter 9: Cultural Impact of the Financial Crisis

"Blaming speculators as a response to financial crisis goes back at least to the Greeks. It's almost always the wrong response." - Lawrence Summers, economist

Whenever there is a major economic event in the United States, and the rest of the world, its impact reverberates for a generation. Anyone who lived through this global financial crisis will recall it many decades later because they saw how it impacted governments, institutions, families and individuals.

The biggest impact probably lies in the housing market. While the United States housing market is on the road to recovery, things are unlikely to ever be the same again. People are a lot more cautious when they think about buying a home, especially if they are young and do not have a ton of savings in the bank. Similarly, there is much more caution associated with taking out a second mortgage or any other type of loan against a home. People now know that their home's value is fleeting. If it is $100,000 one year, it could easily fall to $60,000 or $70,000 a few years later.

In terms of housing, the impact varies based on the city and state where you live. For example, the San Francisco housing market is definitely booming. It has already passed the high levels of 2005 and 2006. However, other cities and states are not as lucky. In Las Vegas, the housing market is at 62 percent of its peak from 2005, while cities such as Philadelphia and Chicago hover at around 70 to 80 percent.

Even in cities such as San Francisco where the market is booming, it represents a new set of problems related to affordability.

As the market booms, housing and apartment prices go up. This means fewer people are able to afford to live near where they work. It results in either longer commutes, or more people sharing homes and apartments with friends or family. The trend of and increased number of people in their 20s living with their parents is not going away anytime soon, because rent prices are too high, especially in major cities.

Another cultural impact of the crisis revolves around public perception. While we go into detail about why the financial bailouts of 2008 and 2009 were necessary to revive the world's failing economy, the public perception is somewhat different. Many people believe that the United States government prioritized saving a few financial institutions over helping the wide majority of its citizens. Not only does this feeling breed a distrust of Wall Street, but it also increases people's distrust and dislike of the government.

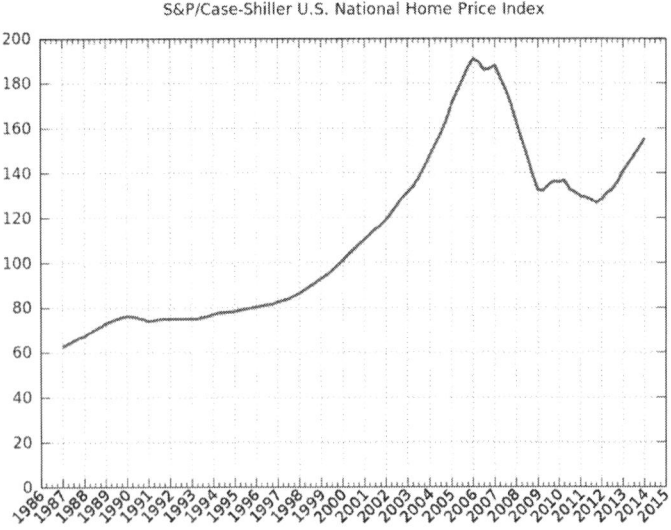

Figure – Case-Shiller Home Price Index 1987 to 2014

Understanding the Financial Crisis of 2008

When the world economy fails, the following years are always difficult. Not only do people have a hard time finding jobs and rebuilding their lives, but governments all over the world must make spending cuts. Often times, these spending cuts result in limited funding for public arts. In 2009, a major survey was conducted in 21 major nations throughout the world. This study discovered that around 13 of the 21 countries were actively engaging in budget cuts for arts, culture and heritage organizations throughout their nations. Out of the nations surveyed, 11 stated that they deemed budget cuts were an absolute necessity following the crisis while another nine said that subsidies for arts and culture organizations were no longer financially feasible.

What happened in 2007 and 2008 may have impacted the United States housing market and the world financial markets with the greatest force, but that impact is felt in every facet of our lives. Whether you feel that impact by looking across the street at a foreclosed home, or by visiting a community arts center that no longer has the funding it used to enjoy, we all experience the consequences of the actions of our governments, mortgage lenders and the major financial institutions on Wall Street.

Chronology of Events

2007:

This is when the housing crisis began, with many individuals and families unable to meet their mortgage requirement thanks to the shift in interest rates on adjustable-rate mortgages. Also, the housing market began to see a gradual decline in housing prices, which further exacerbated the situation with mortgages.

February 2007: Freddie Mac says they will stop buying the riskiest subprime loans.

April 2007: New Century Financial files for bankruptcy. They were a subprime mortgage lender.

July 2007: Bear Stearns, an investment bank, liquidates their two major hedge funds because of the amount of money they invested in risky securities and subprime mortgages.

August 2007: American Home Mortgage Investment, a company responsible for giving out many adjustable-rate mortgages, files for bankruptcy.

August 2007: Fitch Ratings, a credit rating company, decided to cut Countrywide Financial's credit rating to one of its lowest marks, highlighting how much trouble that company was in.

2008:

The United States and its financial markets are in a full-blown recession. The credit markets are majorly impacted by what is going on with the subprime mortgages, and this has a domino impact on other businesses and investments.

January 2008: Bank of America buys Countrywide Financial for $4 billion.

March 2008: The Federal Reserve makes a decision to guarantee $30 billion of the assets of Bear Stearns. This is part of a deal that allowed the government to sponsor the sale of Bear Stearns to JP Morgan Chase.

July 2008: IndyMac Federal Bank is now the largest regulated thrift that fails, leading to seizures by Federal regulators.

September 2008:

Fannie Mae and Freddie Mac are taken over by the United States government.

Bank of America decides to buy Merrill Lynch for $50 billion.

Lehman Brothers files for bankruptcy, marking the end of this financial institution.

AIG takes a bailout from the United States government of around $85 billion, which gives the U.S. government an 85 percent stake in AIG.

Goldman Sachs and Morgan Stanley, two of the largest investment banks in the world, now become bank holding companies. This means they are subject to heightened government regulation.

Washington Mutual Bank closes, with its assets sold to JP Morgan Chase at a knockdown price. This is the largest bank failure in the history of the United States.

There is hope for a $700 billion bailout of Wall Street, but this is rejected in Congress on the 29th of September 2008. The DOW falls a further 800 points on the news.

A few days later, Congress passes a TARP bank bailout package that is signed by President Bush.

Three motor companies, Ford, General Motors and Chrysler all speak with the United States Congress and request a federal loan as part of the bailout package.

Citigroup is rescued by the Treasury Department and the Federal Reserve. There are a number of guarantees and regulations placed on Citigroup as a result of this agreement.

In December 2008, the United States Treasury finally agreed to loans of around $14 billion for General Motors and $4 billion for Chrysler.

Glossary of Financial Terms

Adjustable-Rate Mortgages: A mortgage where the initial interest rate is often lower than the interest rate that kicks in after a certain period of time (one to five years).

Balance of Payments: A summary of all the transactions between a country's residents and nonresidents, which include income, goods or services.

Bank of England: The central bank of the United Kingdom, which plays a similar role as the Federal Reserve in the United States.

Bank of International Settlements: A Swiss bank that helps improve the cooperation and dealings between central banks around the world.

Bankruptcy: Legal proceedings involving a person or business who can no longer afford to pay back their existing debts.

Bloomberg: A global news provider that specializes in news about the financial markets and economics.

Bonds: A type of debt investment where an investor loans money to a company for a definite period of time in return for a variable or fixed interest rate.

Capital Account: This account shows the net worth of a nation or business in relation to their financial dealings and investments.

Capital Requirements: This signifies how much liquid cash a bank must have in relation to their total assets.

Central Bank: This entity is responsible for handling a country's monetary policy. Federal Reserve in America – Bank of England in the United Kingdom.

Collateralized Debt Obligation: A combination of different debt assets pooled together in order to sell to investors. Assets often include mortgages and loans.

Consumer Confidence: This signifies how optimistic or pessimistic people are about the nation's immediate economic future.

Credit Default Swap: A transfer that allows two parties to swap the potential credit exposure of a mortgage or other type of loan.

Credit Union: A non-profit financial institution where members can borrow money at low-interest rates for a variety of reasons.

Current Account: A current account is the sum of a county's balance of trade, net income from foreign countries and the net current transfers. It is essentially the checking account of a country.

Deposit Insurance Limit: This is how much of your money is insured by the United States government's Federal Deposit Insurance Corporation, or FDIC. The amount is currently at $250,000 per bank account.

Derivatives: These are securities that have a price which is based on the underlying assets of the derivative. Derivatives are usually derived from stocks, bonds, currencies or commodities.

DOW Jones: The price-weighted average of the top thirty most significant stocks trading on the New York Stock Exchange.

Economic Bubble: An economic cycle where you see a great deal of expansion, such as companies growing exponentially and stock prices rising very quickly. Almost always followed by a contraction.

Fannie Mae and Freddie Mac: These are government sponsored enterprises that bought mortgages from banks, credit unions and other institutions so that those companies could lend more money to people buying homes.

Financial Guarantors: A person or institution that pledges to pay someone else's debt in the event that they are no longer able to meet their obligations.

Financial Instruments: Any type of tradable asset.

Foreclosure: The process that involves a bank or other institution taking over someone's home because they can no longer keep up with the mortgage payments.

Foreign Exchange Market: This is a decentralized market where foreign currencies are traded on an almost 24-hour a day basis.

Fortune Global 500: A ranking of the top 500 companies in the world based on their revenues. The list is made by the popular *Fortune* magazine.

FTSE 100: This is a list of major blue-chip stocks that are trading on the London Stock Exchange. It is a good representation of the country's current economic climate.

GDP: Gross Domestic Product, or GDP, is the monetary value of all goods and services that are made within a country during a set period of time – usually one year. GDP is calculated both yearly and quarterly, with many economists comparing cross-year GDPs in order to gauge a country's economic health.

Glass-Steagall Act: This was a bill passed in the 1930s by the United States Congress following the Great Depression. The bill took aim at major financial companies and made it against the law for a company to have any interaction between their commercial banking and investment banking sides. The idea was to ensure that the commercial banks took on less risky investments in the future.

Government Deficit: A deficit for your government means that it is spending more money than it brings in from taxation. For some countries, such as Greece, it is a sign of economic trouble. For others, such as the United States, it may be a sign that the country is a safe place for foreigners to invest their money.

Government-Sponsored Enterprises: These are financial services companies that are created and sponsored by the government, but they are not officially a part of the government. Fannie Mae and Freddie Mac are popular examples, although they are now officially owned by the government following the 2008 financial crisis.

Great Depression: A severe economic depression that occurred in October 1929 and continued until the late 1930s. The United States and several other countries suffered from high unemployment and a drastic reduction in economic output.

Hedge Fund: A partnership of different investors where high-risk methods are used in order to gain higher yields. These funds often take undue risks with investors' money, such as investing them into mortgage-backed securities.

High Yield Investments: These are financial investments, usually in stocks, bonds or other assets, that are promising high returns on a quarterly and yearly basis.

Interbank Market: This is a foreign exchange market that comprises of the very top banks from around the world. These banks can exchange currencies with each other in a direct manner, or through an electronic system.

Interest Rates: This is a fraction of a loan that is charged to the person borrowing the loan. The purpose of interest rates is to give lenders an incentive to lend money when taking into account the risk of the borrower defaulting on the loan. Borrowers with worse credit usually have to take on loans with higher interest rates.

Investment Banks: Banks that buy a large number of shares that are recently issued by companies. These banks then sell these shares to other investors and make huge profits by being the middle-men.

Liquidity: How quickly a person, institution or country can get access to cash. Liquidity also refers to how much activity is going on in an economy.

Mortgage Broker: This is a middle-man or intermediary who brings together mortgage borrowers and lenders in order to facilitate deals between them.

Mortgage Company: These are institutions such as banks and credit unions that give out mortgages to borrowers.

Mortgage-Backed Securities: And asset-backed security that is secured through one or more mortgages. The idea is to group mortgages together into one security and then have ratings agencies give them a rating to allow investors to assess the risk associated with investing in a particular security.

NASDAQ: The Nasdaq Composite, which is made up of more than 3,000 technology stocks. Examples are Apple, Alphabet (Google) and Amazon.

New York Stock Exchange: This is the oldest stock exchange in the United States, and it is where a vast majority of the country's trading takes place. Largest stock exchange in the world.

Off-Balance Sheet Financing: This is a type of financing that a company does not put on their balance sheet. An example is an operating lease, where a company takes equipment or other items on loan for a relatively short period of time.

Predatory Lending: Actions carried out by lenders that are unfair or deceptive in nature. These actions are designed to entice borrowers to put themselves in agreements that are not in their best interests.

Quantitative Easing: A move by the central bank that adds new money into a country's money supply.

Ratings Agencies: These companies are responsible for the rating of financial instruments in order to inform investors about the riskiness of a particular investment. For example, something that has a AAA rating means that it is incredibly secure. Whereas a C rating is a sign of an insecure financial instrument.

Recession: A significant period of economic downturn, where there is a decline in activity across the majority of industries. Production, employment, and income all decline during recessions.

Securities: These are financial instruments that take the form of stocks, bonds or options.

Shadow Banking: In simple terms, these are institutions that behave just like banks, but they are not supervised or regulated like banks. In the crisis, they were responsible for starting the trend of turning mortgages into mortgage-backed securities

Subprime Mortgage: This is a type of mortgage given to people who have a credit score of below 600.

U.S. Federal Reserve: The United States' central bank.

U.S. SEC: The Securities and Exchange Commission, or SEC, is responsible for regulating the financial sector in order to protect investors.

United States Home Construction Index: A traded index that is comprised of many different stocks and assets that pertain to the home construction industry.

United States National Economic Stabilization Act of 2008: The economic stimulus packaged that was agreed by the U.S. government to help out banks and other institutions that suffered during the 2007-2008 Financial Crisis.

Acknowledgments

I would like to thank Ansser Sadiq for help in preparation of this book. The quotes are from the Brainy Quotes website. Unless otherwise noted, all the photographs are from the public domain.

Further Reading

Lewis, M. *The Big Sort- Inside the Doomsday Machine.* W.W. Norton& Company Ltd. 2010.

Sorkin, A. *Too Big to Fail – The Inside Story of How Wall Street and Washington Fought to Save the Financial System – and Themselves*. Penguin Books. 2010.

West, D. *– The Great Depression – A Short History*. C&D Publications. 2016.

About the Author

Aiden Young is a writer living Miami, Florida with his wife.

Figure – Aiden Young (photo by Karina Cinnante)

Additional Books by Aiden Young

The Lewis and Clark Expedition – A Short History

The Inventor Thomas Edison – A Short Biography

Donuts: A Sweet Mantra

Index

Symbols

2008 Financial Crisis 7, 51

A

adjustable-rate mortgage
  ARM 4, 10, 21, 24
American Home Mortgage Investment 41
Ameriquest 22

B

Bear Stearns 25, 41, 42
Bernanke, Ben 7, 8
Bush, George 29

C

Carter, Jimmy 3
Chicago 37
Chrysler 43
Citigroup 20, 30, 43
collateralized debt obligation
  CDO 17
Countrywide Financial 21, 41, 42
credit default swap
  CDS 11, 12

F

Fannie Mae 4, 20, 26, 42, 47, 48
Federal Deposit Insurance Corporation
 FDIC 46
Ford 43
Fournier, Ron 23
Freddie Mac 4, 20, 26, 41, 42, 47, 48

G

GDP 2, 8, 13, 33, 47
Geithner, Timothy 3
General Motors 43
Glass-Steagal Act 4
government-sponsored enterprises
 GSE 19
Gramm – Leach – Bliley Act 4
Great Depression 1, 48, 53
Greece 48

I

IndyMac Federal Bank 42

K

Krugman, Paul 3, 20, 30

M

Merill Lynch 26
mortgage 1, 5, 6, 9, 10, 15, 16, 19, 20, 21, 22, 23, 24, 25, 27, 30, 37, 39,
 41, 45, 46, 47, 48, 49, 50

N

National Economic Stabilization Act 26, 51
National Public Radio
 NPR 16
New Century Financial 24, 41
New York Stock Exchange 29, 46, 49

P

Philadelphia 37

S

San Francisco 37
Securities and Exchange Commission
 SEC 4, 5, 51
Skousen, Mark 19
St. Germain Depository Institutions Act 4

U

United States 1, 3, 4, 5, 7, 9, 15, 16, 17, 20, 23, 25, 26, 27, 28, 29, 33, 34, 35, 37, 38, 39, 41, 42, 43, 45, 46, 48, 49, 51

W

Wall Street iii, 1, 2, 3, 4, 22, 28, 29, 30, 33, 34, 35, 38, 39, 42, 53
Washington Mutual Bank 42

Made in the USA
Columbia, SC
04 January 2024